SMOKE

Poems by Ashlee Haze

Copyright © 2020, 2023 by Ashlee Haze

All rights reserved. This book or any portion thereof may not be reproduced or used in any manner whatsoever without the express written permission of the publisher except for the use of brief quotations in a book review. For permission requests, write to the publisher, addressed "Attention: Permissions Coordinator," at the email address below:
info@ashleehaze.com

Printed in the United States of America
Philosophy Media Group,
Second Edition, Revised

Editor: Kaci Diane

Cover Art By: Asia Samson

we are all surviving something.

Table of Contents

foreword	9
where there's smoke	13
things I have set ablaze	15
a bop for a house fire	16
tank	17
alarm	18
multiple choice	19
a poet's ode to her honda civic	20
rescue	21
warriors	23
temple	24
self-reclamation in 3 parts	25
ode to fuckbois	27
hymn	29
the subtle art of missing a fuckboi	31
haiku 1107	33
haiku 1109	34
on delayed gratification	35
otw	36
ash	37
monologue for a magician	39
haiku 1004	41
pillar	42
when you have forgotten int'l players anthem day	43

fault	44
and what am I supposed to do with these free drink coupons?	45
brave new world	46
prodigal	47
haiku 514	48
air	49
clown	51
a star for a war like ours	52
texts I almost sent my ex-boyfriend	54
haiku 915	55
affirmation for a fatherless father	56
natural selection	57
autobiography	58
ghazal for desire	61
a dream in which I am present in my own body	62
haiku 1029	64
lucid	65
multitudes	66
bequeath	67
epilogue	69
antidote	71
Acts of Accountability for Anyone Who's Ever Hurt Someone	73
Acts of Self-Care after a Relationship Transitions	74
Acts of Self-Care for a Big Girl (or anybody, really)	75
collected poems from previous works	79

this spot just won't come out	81
shake what the motherland gave you	82
the origin of a monster	83
for colored girls who don't need Katy Perry when Missy Elliott is enough	84
The Help	86
Lazarus	88

foreword

On June 21, 2018, I had just come home from a five-month tour to my partner of ten years insisting upon meeting me in public to talk. That night, in a dimly lit Applebee's booth, he gulped down a Long Island and simply replied "yes" when I asked if someone was pregnant. You could say I had a hunch.

Before his admission, I had it all figured out. If he were cheating and had gotten another woman pregnant, it would not be my problem. I'd given myself and my friends the pep talk. I told them I didn't care. We were barely holding on anyway, and he was free to do what he wanted. I would say goodbye to him and be on my way.

Every lie I ever told was an attempt to avoid grief—this was no exception.

I avoided grief by attempting to be friends with a man who was still deceiving me. I threw myself into my work and read a myriad of self-help books. When that didn't work, I attacked him. I attempted to control him. I refused to let him pretend to be a good guy and get away with what he had done. I tried to force him into accountability and quickly learned that you cannot bully someone into love. I also learned that my relationship with love is directly related to my relationship with forgiveness. I realized that I could only forgive him and forgive myself by telling my truth. To do that, I had to let grief in.

So I did. I gave myself permission to be angry, sad, and confused; to be weak and defeated; to need help from others; to be tender and brokenhearted. *Smoke* is a collection of poems written over the course of two years. It is my account of what it feels like to be intimate with sadness and loneliness. It is a portrait of grief and the courage it takes to sit with it as well as a portrait of healing a process to which I remain committed. *Smoke* is a documentation of growth and its grueling process. I have accepted that I cannot prevent heartbreak—I have a feeling this won't be my last. I can practice healing, though. I can choose love and courage.

In the midst of this great personal loss, I was also suffering professionally. Poetry Slam, Inc—an organization I also spent ten years with—had suffered a significant loss and ceased to exist. My world was changing rapidly, and grief was getting comfortable. I had some very difficult decisions to make. The choice I am most proud of is my decision to stay in the paint and continue creating and working.

I want to thank those who witnessed my heartbrokenness and did not judge me for it. I am grateful to those who sat with me, talked to me, and checked in. To the homies—Hunter, Contessa, Alvin, Kenny, and Corey—I am ever grateful to be chosen by you. To my sister Shanel, thank you for always defending my honor and making space for me. To my emotional partner Pam, thank you for your commitment and partnership. To my coach Chauncey, thank you for bringing me the light and reminding me of my power. To my mom, godfather, GG, and Will thank you for your unconditional love. To the Atlanta poetry community, thank you for being my home. To my brothers—you are the brightest among us. I hope you are proud to call me sister. To Andrea Gibson and Asia Samson, thank you for seeing me as an artist and a human. It is an honor to be mentored by you.

I am grateful for the work of bell hooks, Brene Brown, Don Miguel Ruiz, Katherine Woodward Thomas, Eckhart Tolle, Marshall Rosenberg, and Paulo Coelho. I am grateful for the sacred texts and their teachings.

I am grateful to every person who has experienced my work and shared space with me. I am grateful to be trusted as a storyteller and a representative. I remain committed to this work and to love.

On January 22, 2019, eight days before my 30th birthday, my ex-partner welcomed twins into the world while I prepared to begin my 3rd spring of touring as a performance poet. I have since allowed myself room for grief and gratitude. At the time of this book's press, we remain out of contact with each other. I wish him a life of love and joy.

where there's smoke

after "things that shine in the night" by Rigoberto Gonzalez

things I have set ablaze

the blunt, unceremoniously
my heart, a groundless sacrifice of the most bloody thing I could offer
the blunt, this time, with reverence to the ritual
the whites of my eyes, for all the ways they betrayed me
the loins, scraping match against box as if to excavate a summer out of myself
fear, writhing still at the stake
the part of me that cares what other people think
depression, a flair you can't see until you're right up on it
and once, a home I still wanted to live in

a bop for a house fire

my mother taught me how to be
a woman. how to sear the meat and make
the dirty laundry disappear. so when you showed up
ready to build a house, I brought secrets to mix
in with the foundation. that's how I learned to make
a home. by hiding the ugliest parts.

trouble don't last always.

my daddy left me his ability to even a score. I learned
early how dangerous a wounded man can be. watched him
shrink everything in the house to make himself giant. there
was love, though. on the days when they remembered the vows and
the good ol days. my parents gave to me from half empty
cups when it was all they had. forgive me for never being full.
I didn't learn until later the value of an unpretty truth. no one
gave me permission to be the spectrum of myself.

trouble don't last always.

it is all gone, now. we have since forgiven the debts. this
lot is no longer ours and to that I say amen. although
we torched the walls and their whispers, we made it
out alive. we tried to save it. remodeled the best we could.
sometimes disaster swallows even the best intentions. praise God we
know what not to do now. praise the universe for the chance to build
again.

trouble don't last always.

tank

the old folks say
when you dream of fish
someone in the village is pregnant

when you left
your ghost sat beside me as I
dreamt koi
and I woke up to an empty womb

bless the ancestors
for revealing truth to me
even in my sleep

bless the great beyond
for the ways in which it
reminds me that light
will always slice through the dark

alarm

"he's coming"
I say to passersby
as they witness my consumption

surely a man wouldn't
cause a fury like that
and leave me to inhale the fumes

by the time I even smelled smoke
you were on the other side of town
with your hands full

too occupied to be bothered with
my screams
too busy to put out
my fire

multiple choice

when my options are:
    a. call the cops
    b. call my cousins 'nem
    c. risk him punching something other than the wall/
       breaking something other than my phone
I hesitate, still.
the correct answer doesn't jump out at me- at least not the way he does.

I dial 911 in terror.
which am I more afraid of?
    a. what he'll do to me?
    b. what they'll do to him?
trick question.
I am a black woman experiencing violence by the hands of a black man
every day is a test to see how much I suffer to keep him safe.

after "a rapper's ode to his Honda Civic" by Adan Bean

a poet's ode to her honda civic

when you realize
it has been a year
since he abandoned the old honda
do not be surprised
for it is not beyond him
to get something new and shiny
and not even bother to discard
what has served him until this point

my dear honda,
you deserve at least a proper burial
you are more than just storage for shit
he has no use for anymore
more than just a wasteland for spills
he couldn't bother to clean up

I don't believe he intended
to leave you this long. sometimes
new cars require more attention
sometimes you get more than you bargained for

someone is coming for you
a decent man with the tools to
get you running again

if he comes back for you
there will be a price to pay
you may be old
but you are worth something
whether he knows it or not

rescue

warriors

when the revolution comes
send me women who smoke
and drink gin
and cuss
send me women who sit with their legs open
messy haired women
who cock pistols for sport
send me women in comfortable shoes
women who change tires and check the oil
then tell the tow truck man to keep it moving
cuz he took too long
[ain't it just like a man to take too long]
send me women who roll backwoods
and know all the verses to the Player's Anthem
send me the village of the unladylike
and watch us save your sorry asses

Published in Poetry Magazine, May 2021

temple

the pastor says
we are having church
and I begin to wonder what it means to
possess a thing you cannot touch

I caught the holy ghost once
after chasing him in the back pews
held on to him long enough to convince my mother of salvation
then went home and set him free in the wild

how pompous of man to
think himself temple
don't you know I have called out to God
in emptier structures?

the doors of the church are open
come, sit
lay your burdens at the altar
eat the body and its crumbs, sip the blood
until you are satisfied

I am unlearning how to erect myself
as a stained-glass home
this pipe organ heart is guilty of calling out to the godless
especially men who peek during prayer

self-reclamation in 3 parts

I
I was told that my body is not my own
it belongs first to God
then to my father
then to the man who he gives me to
my father is dead. so who is the rightful owner of this body now?
I offer my body to my lover as if it is something that is not mine
have you seen how people treat things that are not theirs?

II
I log into Facebook to see another meme
that pictures a scantily clad Beyonce side-by-side a headwrap
donning Erykah Badu
asking the question "why be eye candy when you can be soul food?"
like I can't multitask
like I won't get drunk in love then tell you to call Tyrone
like I won't read <u>the coldest winter ever</u> and <u>citizen</u> before lunch
like I didn't twerk across the stage to get my degree
like I didn't write this poem to the tune of Bodak Yellow
like I needed another serving of respectability politics
or another man who can't be bothered with the black woman's
feminism but knows how she ought to conduct herself
like I got time for men who shame black women's sexuality in public
but consume it behind closed doors
let me be clear: ain't nobody got time for that

III
what a time to be woman
the way we show up for ourselves
the way we dare to be visible
the way we snatch our stories back from the men who co-op them

the world is not kind to a woman who is confident in her sexuality
my spirit quakes as I watch my friends explain consent to grown men
then see women shame other women for what they wear
feminism allows you modesty in the same way it allows me to wear whatever I want
I am here as a woman to reclaim all the parts of myself I was ashamed to get to know
to proclaim myself as a woman who is both/and
not either/or
let me be clear, a woman who is only either is still deserving of respect
and as for me and my house
I can be eye candy and soul food
I know how to multitask

ode to fuckbois

O, fuckboi
I marvel at your majesty
the way you sit upon my couch
eating my chips
using my internet
you are a wonder among men

O, fuckboi
I stand in awe of your ways
your propensity to drive the gas
out of yo mama's car
how you leave it empty
you follow through like none other

O, fuckboi
your basicness be amazing
how you don't delete your texts to your ex
how your password be predictable
you ever the same, yesterday, today, and tomorrow

O, fuckboi
you be a miracle worker
the way you manage to not have a house or car
but yet can afford studio time and weed

O, fuckboi
how did I live without you?
why didn't I know I needed someone
to drink all of my Hennesy?

O, fuckboi
have you not anyone to hold you accountable?
forgive me, I forgot you all be cut from the same cloth
whether it be Gucci or dashiki

O, fuckboi

I hold steadfast that you will change
that you allow yourself to be free and tap into your power
but in the meantime
I'm singing protection spells to the tune of
"call Tyrone" and "no scrubs"

O, fuckboi
I have seen the fruit of your labor
how you make a house out of women
and don't even bother to take your shoes off at the door

O, fuckboi
your unhealed trauma is an uninvited guest
that sucks all the joy out of a room
ignoring those wounds will not make them go away any faster

O, fuckboi
I have seen you cower at love and the bravery it requires
how you pile the armor on and dare to call yourself fearless

O, fuckboi
don't you know karma by name?
don't you know the cycle of toxic masculinity as a remedy for pain
can only stop when you make it?

O, fuckboi
my screenshot game strong
so consider this my farewell
stay out of my dms
you can ease on down the road
into the land of far far away

hymn

lean in,
let me tell you of a wall-less church
a congregation of women in the business of saving
women who do the heavy lifting while the world gawks from the sidelines
women given the trash and the broken
yet refused to think you disposable
women serving as a second womb
for the motherless
for grown men intent on not doing their own emotional work
and we let you bask in our greatness
should you be so lucky to be granted the magic
because we might side eye you to kingdom come
might roll our eyes 'til you disappear
and ain't that sorcery?
the way our defenses protect us from elements
from a winter of the undeserving intent getting all of our harvest

you so vain you think we do this for you
as if we wake up in the morning pandering to the world's gaze
as if the women of Alabama and Wakanda had nothing better to do
than to save men from themselves
lean in,
we save ourselves first and you get saved in the process
and ain't that the way it always goes?
we get dressed in all the work we do
and you are saved just by touching the hem of our garments
black queer women create social justice movements
and you make it about people oblivious of their own privilege
men who demand we be black first and women when it suits them
our intersectionality is an inconvenient myth
misogyny is a weed that keeps growing back

no matter how many think pieces we spray on it

the trouble with being the savior, though
is people usually don't think we need saving
don't think we need gentleness
to my sisters, I vow to be gentler with you
know that we are worthy of someone who helps with the work
too long we have dined with the world
serving food from our own gardens
on tables we bought and built

all that I have I owe to black women
I say glory to the women who thought I was worth saving
glory to the women who think I'm enough
even on days when I fall short
I say I see you
you be visible
and you be worthy of all this praise

the subtle art of missing a fuckboi

you do not miss him
you miss his brand of high
this is withdrawal, nothing more

have a seat
take a deep breath
drink a glass of water
do not call him

you know how this ends
you know he will not answer
leave him be
he has already left you

make room for both grief and gratitude
give yourself permission to miss the smell of smoke mixed with his skin
grieve the loss of a home you grew up in
look at the pictures, play the song you danced to on his birthday
but for God's sake do not beg for ambivalence

do not spend winter waiting on the bridge
spend it by a fire, in the warmth of your own love
spend it with those who know a good thing when they see it
those who read all the parts of the paragraphs you sent
those who ain't scared of light or truth
haven't you given enough to the godless?
ain't it time to collect your things?
ain't it time to realize you can't love nobody into loving you?

keep everything you wanted to give him for yourself
be the lover he wasn't brave enough to be

love your way through this
sobriety is a process

haiku 1107

you are drained because
that's not a partner. that's
a liability

haiku 1109

my partner left and
I'm still doing his work. no
wonder I'm exhausted

on delayed gratification

it feels good, don't it?
whatever *it* is
the petty move. the thing you think will
finally make him sorry. or you feel better.
whichever comes first.

the social media post. the busted windshield. the mediocre sex with someone new.
this ain't justice, but it's a drop in the bucket, right?

karma ain't punctual
she moves slowly and settles quietly

you want loud justice. evidence of reconciliation

tell me, though.
do you really want someone you have to bully the truth out of?
remember, there are better wars
and villages of men who show up of their own accord

what would you do with the spoils, anyway?
convince yourself you made the right decision?
ha! any decision you put all your power into is the right one

do not let looking back for him make you salt
there is beauty you're missing on the horizon

otw

I have lived my life
with the promise
that *somebody* is coming
whether to save
or share
or hold me in the still of winter

I understand that loneliness is, indeed, a temporary phenomenon
yet, in this moment
I am aware of the possibility that this could be lasting

who am I if no one is on the way?
what of the little girl in me that peeks through the blinds?
who then to fill the space I been saving, huh?
tell me again, how I must show up for myself
tell me again how foolish of me to desire company
and I will proclaim
I am so full that I don't know what to do with my own running over
what sin have I committed?
to want?
what penance for the audacity to yearn?

I have made room in my new house for multiple truths
yes, I am enough all by my glorious self
yes, I want to share this glory with you

ash

monologue for a magician

I loved a man of many talents
you should see the way he can season a wound
how skillfully he skirts accountability
the way his words and actions never cross paths

he's got a gift for making bad things worse.

once, I watched him take the life we
built and dismantle it piece by piece
he smuggled it out of the back door
moved it to the other side of town

the nigga didn't even leave a note.

that kind of man don't care who he runs over
don't care who gets caught in the crossfire
he's got a knack for being godless
no wonder he ran from me

a conjurer like that knows light when he sees it
he knows stardust and can sniff a warrior out in his sleep
and with sleight of hand he'll suck all the good out of you
if you let him
and if you don't-
if you get out with anything
he'll holler like he's hurt
now ain't that something?
a man who thinks he's a victim of your survival

his best work was done in the medium of gaslight
I thought I was going crazy
but it was just the fumes

I got so dizzy once, I mistook him for an honest man

he almost got me
almost made me think I was responsible for my own suffering
I got out, though. scathed, but breathing.
that's the real magic

haiku 1004

you can pick the white
girl without bruising the black
girl in the process

pillar

Prince died.
we rode around the city
grief so thick
the sound of his guitar couldn't mask it
we bought matching shirts
and watched purple rain in the front row of a packed theater
grateful to be in the room

when Michael went
we could hardly see through our fog
couldn't even talk about it for weeks
but we held each other until life made sense again

then Aretha left
and you were nowhere to be found
I cried in the car still
only this time with an unfamiliar hand to hold

they wonder why I'm salt
I don't know how to tell them I'm looking back
in hopes to catch your gaze through the ruin
I can't tell them I'd be a pillar
to see you one last time

after "when you have forgotten Sunday" by Gwendolyn Brooks

when you have forgotten int'l players anthem day

when you have forgotten the anthem
forgotten to choose me
when you have forgotten the sacred ritual of smoke
while maxing out your subs in an old car
when you have pledged your allegiance to another
forgotten Saturday morning walks
Sunday afternoons in bed as the world outside my window spun
without us
when you have forgotten the movies
how our hands were magnets in a dark theater
the choreography of you eating the rest of the food
off my plate
clumsy Kwanzaas as we conjured home
or something like it
when you have forgotten
California
Florida
Tennessee
me playing my favorite songs on repeat
and cussing you out for playing trap music before noon
when you have forgotten the things worth keeping
then you may tell
then I may believe
you have forgotten me well

fault

in the end
my friends hated you and
with good reason

in my quest for justice
I poured them the hot tea
when our home had become cold

I am not sorry for speaking to those willing to listen
I am sorry that I was not always fair to your side of the story

my friends weren't there
when I was practicing
my best offense
on your ego

my friends did not
take the knife
when it called out to me
like a siren

we are no saints
there will be no stain glass window
erected in remembrance of this

blessed is the woman who learns from her mistakes
blessed is the woman who survives a man who doesn't

and what am I supposed to do with these free drink coupons?

twitter inquires if I intend to boycott Starbucks// I point the loaded question to the ceiling// ask Twitter what I'm supposed to do with all these free drink coupons// ask twitter *if they got coffee money*// I hold justice, who is now kicking, up by the hair and inquire of the hungry mob// is this mine to serve?// twitter don't give a damn about the particulars// wants the roasted head of the company on a platter// twitter forgets to ask the victims how they want their justice cooked// instead, gathers up they cousins 'nem for reckoning// twitter's idea of a safe space// is one where the taxidermy of the convicted line the walls// I am a woman with many shortcomings// I got failures I still need to clean out of the backseat of my car// I wonder how long before I am threatened to be stuffed// what offense I am in proximity to that justifies my own gutting

brave new world

a person who chooses
themself over motherhood
is a gladiator indeed

a person who has lost a child
and attempts again
is a champion

a person who chooses to parent
children they did not birth
is a beacon

a person who uses their power
to allow another to raise their children
is a warrior

these people have won
the biggest fight of all

they have learned to value
their truth over the world's
expectations

that's the most valiant thing on this side of the stars

prodigal

my Mom asks "do you still believe in Jesus?"
she reminds me that he is the way
the truth, and the light
fears I have gone off the path
she paved for me

she is right. I have wandered this
vast earth and found so many tunnels
all with light at the end

I tell her I believe in anything that saves
and brings me closer to God
I remind her that she is a way, too
I believe in *her*

I tell her I have spent my years watching the women I love
save themselves first
and that is my religion

she doesn't always understand
where I go and why
but she prays for me
in Jesus' name

wherever she is
is a place I call home
there is always a feast for me
when I return

haiku 514

I cannot both judge
my mother and love her- I
will choose the latter

air

clown

when the class comedian takes my phone
and puts his number in it
the unhealed pre-teen in me smiles
at the half-assed effort
he must know I got a cabinet full of snacks and a jar full of weed
he must know I learned from generations of women
how to prioritize the needs of black men over my own

you would think I know better
than to walk into the jester's court
fat girl be ripe fruit for the cute, wounded boy who can pull a smile out of your teeth

I give the way a fat girl should
I crack open easy and the nectar seeps into his palms

he pretends to like me for me
I know he is drawn to sticky women with lips like sap

it does not take long for him to miscalculate a lie
messy men always leave a clue behind

I remind him of all the ways he got me fucked up
I remind myself ain't no glory in being the butt of his jokes

after "one last poem for Richard" by Sandra Cisneros

a star for a war like ours

Los Angeles
is the closest we ever came to heaven
we wandered together and unafraid
laughed full bellied
until the valley glowed a brilliant orange
held each other in tiny apartments
that always had enough room for our dreams
and the too many clothes I packed

I'll remember you at your best
with the faint glow of a city filled with angels resting on those
gorgeous eyes

we came "home"
nestled back into the comfort of our cruelty
suffocated our valor with untruth
made kindling of whatever good intentions remained

the smoke has cleared now, all that is left
is a photo you were bent on not smiling for
the dreams that survived
and of course, the wounds
some of which were here before we collided

I figured the least I could offer is this poem-
a star to commemorate the casualties
a prayer that we'll know love
the way we knew it on Hollywood Boulevard

I have since gone back
sat at our table
had sweet sacrament in remembrance of you
it is a pilgrimage I make to honor the slice of holiness we had

you can give whatever you want to whomever you choose to make a home out of
children, promises, even forever
but only I know what you look like against a California sunset
with wind in your hair
your brow unburdened by life

thank you for sitting in the warm sand with me along a begging shore
may God bless the beautiful failures we made
I am grateful to have failed with you
thank you for LA
for the space to be brave enough
to become myself

texts I almost sent my ex-boyfriend

happy birthday/ congratulations/ did you see the moon tonight?/ does she know how much her happiness cost me?/ why?/ I would ask if you are happy but I know happy people don't behave this way/ did you pick my name out of your teeth before you kissed her?/ what will you tell your children? what parts of their origin story will you redact?/ why?/ why?/ answer me dammit/ I'm sorry/ I'm not sorry/ I saw that shit you posted on Facebook/ remember that time we drank milkshakes under the stars? remember all the good intentions we had?/ how's the forgetting going? any tips you'd like to share?/ I am trying to scrub you out of my bones and the stain won't lift/ I learned how to roll a blunt today/ amen/ we never had love. we had nostalgia doused in possession. that's not enough to stay/ I'm not the same woman you left/ amen/ amen/ amen/ was that you driving behind me?/ was that you in the grocery store?/ are the kids alright?/ I dropped something on the ground and had to choose whether it was too soiled to keep. when did you decide this was not worth dusting off?/ the day after you left I messaged the man I told you I wouldn't/ he didn't respond/ amen/ Andre dropped a new verse today/ amen/ amen/ Alex Trebek has died of cancer and I'm not okay/ my therapist says we should expect to grieve for the same amount of time we knew each other. I hope she knows we ain't got time for that/ every day since you left, I count the things I would have done differently. I know by name the wounds I made. I'm so sorry./ please forgive me/ I forgive you/ amen.

haiku 915

I will remember
the time you loved me so much
you let me go free

affirmation for a fatherless father

you are a good father
you are a present father
one that ain't afraid of softness
or tears
or joy
or the truth
you have survived fatherlessness
and dared to brave on despite the scar that left on your heart
any assignment you failed before this
does not define you. choosing this one
giving it all you have to give
is the bravest thing you can do

natural selection

should it happen
that no human climbs out of this body
I will leave behind my will to love
in spite of
see how it breathes
my longing to heal and take care of and make whole
ask me of the poems
and I will show you my children
the tribes I have written
to survive the most unholy wars
ain't that a royal bloodline?
how the words be fit for surviving?
ain't that a kind of motherhood?
to bring something into the world
and not know if the evil will rip it to shreds?

after "my honest poem" by Rudy Francisco

autobiography

my name is Ashlee
my favorite color is purple
and I watch way too much television
like watch entire seasons of baking reality tv shows in a day much television
I believe in wearing leggings as pants
and almost everything I eat ends up somewhere on my clothes
most days, I am too lazy to fold my clothes, so I let them sit in the basket
I don't watch much sports
but I still don't forgive the Falcons for blowing a 28-3 lead in the Superbowl
I work out 3 days a week
and I am still not comfortable saying that without people looking at me like the liar I used to be
I used to be a liar
used to tell myself all the things I would do on Monday
next month
New Year's Day
but now I believe in todays
I don't understand grape-flavored things
because they never taste like grapes
I think Coke canceling Sprite Remix is one of the biggest tragedies of my generation
my father died when I was 22 years old
I have finally forgiven God for that
I have survived the type of heartbreak that makes monsters out of men, yet
I chose softness
I chose healing

I chose love
I chose to open my heart again
I have learned to care less about what people think
and learned to walk in my truth
that's the most gangsta shit I'll ever do
a man made a mess of me he couldn't clean up
then black women and queer folks stepped in to help me finish the job
and if that ain't a metaphor
then this ain't a poem about courage
a poem about a girl who could have clocked out but didn't
a poem about how life knocked the wind out of me and my village
showed up to nurse me back to health
about how much I have lost and lost and lost and got the nerve to still be standing
dammit I'm magic
I'm also human and flawed
I have let pain do the talking where love should have
I am still forgiving myself for that
I am the person
who skips a song ever time
but refuses to take it off the playlist
if my life were a playlist
it would start with Stevie Wonder
and end with the Goo Goo Dolls "Iris"
there would be much Justin Timberlake
Sade, Jill Scott
and Cardi B
there would be 3 different versions of Hotel California
and my mother's favorite spiritual
people ask what I do for a living, I say
I am a storyteller
and the one that has become my favorite to tell so far
is my own

ghazal for desire

tell me of the cavity you have made of your sweet dreams.
display proudly the safe bets, the familiar, the neat dreams.

perfection is where shame builds a glass house on a green hill.
reveal the fragmented plans of the bare incomplete dreams.

watch how you shrink at the begging question *what do you want?*
hold space for the whole of you, praise even the petite dreams.

sit at the table and let the milk drip from the round mouth.
over-running cup, pomegranate, honey-dipped feast dreams.

you wild and feral child, let your yearning be unabashed
how fragile your want, carefully watch the way you treat dreams.

play me the mixtape of your forgotten longing and desire.
the bass wonders into daring revery, the beat dreams.

I petition the God[s] to hear the wailing of my heart.
may Haze be a woman, who, in the midst of defeat, dreams.

a dream in which I am present in my own body

I have spent my life
living as a ghost
in the shell of a woman
in reverie, I exist in a space where I am present in my own body
and here it does not belong to anyone but me
this body, an erasure poem
void of the praise I would not give it
is now a place I dwell

here, I name all my body parts
and there are no bad words
here, I am the rule and not the exception
here, my fat is not sacrilege
is only decoration for a home I am proud to live in
here, in this wonderland,
my flesh is not carved or covered in a quest for approval
I give myself permission to be
and it is all that matters
in this paradise, I commune with myself
and no one names it sin
I realize how willingly I have named myself damned
and how hesitant I have been to name myself god

this body be a hallelujah
it is a church,
holy and unscathed,
a trembling indigo morning
that I worship
when everyone is looking

oh, universe
if I cannot manifest this existence

let this sleep be an endless one
let me lead a life in any realm
that allows me to show up as myself

haiku 1029

I am more than a
snack—I be a whole banquet
bring your appetite

lucid

and there, along the perimeter, is a dreamscape in which
all that I desire finds me
these walls, made of the breath of all my beloved
the dust and glitter of a favorite song, my mama's rice and gravy
floors lined with
the laughing kind of teeth
this holy space feels much like a beach
free of every nigga who didn't text me back
the air smells like something mutual
tastes like doing what I love and being visible in the doing

multitudes

we contain multitudes
we weep
fight
know grief like an old lover
we play cards and talk shit
we play the dozens- with boundaries
cuz I'm gone say something about yo mama
but you say something about mine I'll be ready to fight
we throw shade about the potato salad
we footwork and juke
we eat fish and spaghetti
we fail but make the trying look good
we hide Aunt Annie's wig
scrape up a dollar to go to the candy lady
ask daddy even after mama just told us no
we steal a piece of Sunday dinner before it's cooled off
burn our mouths and still come back for more
we be a scorched people
who know the heat of fire
and live always to tell the story

bequeath

it has been a year
and I have finally gotten the courage to go back to our favorite restaurant
this time—I only order what I like
the way I like it

there is a couple in our booth
they remind me so much of us
all afro puffs and baby dreads
all sit on my side so I can hold your hand under the table
all ordering and making plans to eat each other's food
all teeth and dimples and grinnin' like it's Sunday in Atlanta
and if you act right
we might can order two appetizers
and God done gave us this day
and this bread
and this love
and we got ice cream at the house
and another season left of the Wire to watch
and new weed
and old music

and I smile cuz I know they still got tomorrow
these brilliant brown babies
have time to break and mend
and choose each other again
they got joy and a new booth with their names on it
and I think to myself *it's in good hands*

I take my food to-go

pray they do this like communion
I pray wherever you are
you still eat good on Sundays

epilogue

on the cusp of fall, I met a man with a name sweet as Louisiana
brown butter beautiful and brilliant as Saturday afternoon
we loved like we'd been practicing
like the years made us wiser without taking the softness

we black and brilliant and together
we debate politics and music
we loved like we done got good at it

one Sunday in January, before winter could get comfortable in our bones
I reached for him and he did not reach back
and that is how the story ends this time.
not in drama or tragedy, but in romance.

in this one, I do not make a scene.
I exit stage left and send for my things later.
I eat sushi for a week. I call my sister and cry.
but I do not spend the spring begging to be loved.

if I have learned anything, it is not to chase ghosts.
this is an exercise in love, too.
learning to let go of someone when they decide to let go of you.

antidote

Acts of Accountability for Anyone Who's Ever Hurt Someone

1. Apologize as soon as you are aware of the harm you've caused.
2. Respect any boundary the person you've harmed sets. Do not harm them again with your presence.
3. If the recipient of harm consents to your presence, do not harm them more with your distance.
4. Offer to make amends. Respect their right to decline. Respect their right to define what an amend is.
5. Understand the difference between consequences and punishment. You should accept consequences. You should not accept punishment. Harm is not a remedy for harm.
6. Identify your own wounds. Heal them. This is solely your responsibility.
7. Demonstrate your understanding of your harm through your deeds. Love is as love does, not as love says.
8. Forgive yourself. This is the only forgiveness you are entitled to.

Acts of Self-Care after a Relationship Transitions

1. Get rid of things your ex-partner/person left. You may keep gifts, so long as they still serve you.
2. Make a mixtape for yourself. Sad songs. Ratchet Songs.
3. Cry without judging your sadness.
4. Scream without becoming victim to your anger.
5. Look in the mirror. Tell the person you see they are not defined by someone else's departure.
6. Invite your friends over. Share space with those who choose you.
7. Write. Letters (not to send, but to document), journal entries, poems, songs.
8. Laugh. This is the most rebellious thing you can do.

This is how we make room for love—by clearing out all that is not love. This is how we make room for grace—by being gracious to ourselves.

Acts of Self-Care for a Big Girl (or anybody, really)

1. Buy a new piece of clothing. One with the tag still on it. Try it on. Make sure it is what you want for your body as it is right now, not as you wish it were.
2. Look in the mirror. Tell the woman you see that she is enough. Tell her she is worthy just as she is.
3. Dance to your favorite song. Bonus points for doing this naked.
4. Prepare a meal for yourself. Whatever you want. No judgement. No guilt.
5. Get a massage/ facial/hair done/nails done/ *everything did*
6. Touch yourself. Explore your own terrain.

This is how we show others how to take care of us. By taking care of ourselves first. This is how we teach others to accept us. By accepting ourselves first.

Search for Ashlee Haze on Spotify & Apple Music for exclusive playlists

collected poems from previous works

this spot just won't come out

my father died
and every morning I wake up with grief outstretched
covering me like an extra blanket
grief dripping down the walls
grief rising from my clothes like cheap perfume
grief stuck under my shoes like stepped-in gum
grief in the crevices of my teeth
grief spilled on the rug I just bought
this grief--
this rugged thing--
it is ugly all over
and I got it all over everything

shake what the motherland gave you

he says "real women don't twerk."
oh really? the last time I checked, what I do with my backside
don't make me hold my head any less high
I remember before you called it twerkin'
me and my cousins would "pop" in the backyard at family reunions
and it didn't make us any less women
I remember watching my mother and her sisters move their hips
like there was freedom in their bones and it didn't make them any
less goddess
we have been shaking our backsides since before we knew what
foreign soil tasted like
back home, called it mapouka, called it kukere
called it sacrifice for the gods
and I will present my offering every time I hear
"cash money records taking over for the 99 and the two thousand"
I will not let you tell me that the Africa in my back is something that I
should be ashamed of
I will not let you tell me that I should quiet these drums
I will display them for all the world to see
they are mine
they are mine
they are mine.

the origin of a monster

the little boy who breaks the toy he is told he cannot have
or punches the little girl that beats him in a race
grows up to be the man who stabs a woman who refuses his advances
he is the "nice kid" you laughingly told your friends
just wouldn't take no for an answer
and sometimes he grows up to become president

for colored girls who don't need Katy Perry when Missy Elliott is enough

3rd grade. I'm in the hallway, when I'm sure I shouldn't have been and Cory White comes up to me and asks, "Yo! Have you heard that new Missy Elliott track?"
I reply, "Who is Missy Elliot!?!"
at the time my parents only let me listen to the gospel and the smooth jazz station
but that day... I went home, ran upstairs to my room
and closed the door (a cardinal sin in a black mother's house)
and waited on TRL to come on
then it happened. metallics and a black trash bag fill my TV screen
and I hear the coolest thing I'd ever heard in 8 years of living
beep beep, who got the keys to my jeep... Vrooooommm!
at that moment I had my entire life figured out
I was going to grow up to be Missy Elliott
I spent the next ten years of my life recording and rewinding videos to learn dance moves
passing that dutch, getting my freak on
and trying to figure out what the hell she was saying in work it
there were so many artists I could have idolized at the time
but Missy was the only one who looked like me
It is because of Melissa Elliott
that I believed that a fat black girl from Chicago
could dance until she felt pretty
could be sexy and cool
could be a woman playing a man's game
and be unapologetic about it
if you ask me why representation in the media is important
I will show you my velour outfit and the matching Kangol hat I begged my parents for
I will show you a woman who learned to dance until she felt pretty

feminism wears a throwback jersey, bamboo earrings, and a face beat for the gods
feminism is Da Brat, Missy, Lil Kim, Angie Martinez, and Left Eye on the "Not Tonight" track
feminism says as a woman in my arena you are not my competition
as a woman in my arena your light doesn't make mine any dimmer

Dear Missy,
I did not grow up to be you, but I did grow up to be me
and to be in love with who this woman is
to be a woman playing a man's game
and not be apologetic about any of it
If you ask me why representation is important
I will tell you that on the days I don't feel pretty
I hear the sweet voice of Missy singing to me
pop that pop that, jiggle that fat/ don't stop, get it til your clothes get wet
I will tell you that right now there are a million
black girls just waiting to see someone who looks like them

The Help

"you is smart, you is kind, you is important."
I am in my sophomore film class
when my white professor reasons that
"Black women across America should be outraged at the depiction of maids in the new film 'The Help.'"
I think to myself "outraged about what?"
the only people ever offended by the truth are those when given the choice prefer the lie
I find this movie to be mildly nostalgic
it reminds me of my grandmother who cleaned houses by day and was a Chicago hotel maid by night
reminds me of my mother showing me pictures of her grandmother's house in Mississippi
the floors shined even in the photographs
she reminds me
"we didn't have much, but it was always clean"
it reminds me of Saturday mornings spent earning my right to go outside
back when children had to earn their right to go outside
"Are the baseboards clean!?" my mother would ask
as if anyone but her ever noticed a dirty baseboard anyway
it reminds me that cleanliness is next to godliness
and I have the blood of broom toting angels flowing through my veins
WHAT WERE YOU EXPECTING?
this ain't no Ancestry.com commercial
this is the story of history at it's finest
the story of women who kept their prayers in their apron pockets
and sprinkled them in dinner so the children they raised would know love even after they were gone
women who knew 101 ways to use Crisco
women who knew school as somewhere they'd been once upon a time but could never go back

because 90 cents an hour kept bellies full and clothes on backs
what upsets me is that you, like too many people I know
think that this history is something to be ashamed of
it's ok to be from any other chapter in the history book
but you be cursed if you be this
my knowledge of my ancestors may only span 200 years
but I am proud to be the daughter of Mississippi maids and Birmingham martyrs
you laugh at our grandmothers for getting this language wrong
they were just trying to make do with the stolen pieces they were given

on May 6, 2012 I graduated from Georgia State University
and it was a testament to the women who came before me
who cleaned houses so that I wouldn't have to
who served coffee quietly so that I could be a poet
it was for Geraldine Harris, Ophelia McGinnis, Aunt Essy, Aunt Katie, Aunt Annie
so they would know I don't take anything they've done for granted
what makes me mad
is that you make fun of the mantra my grandmother's spirit speaks to me every day
"You is smart, you is kind, and doggone it you is important."

Lazarus

when Lazarus fell sick Mary and Martha ran to Jesus to tell him the news.
they were expecting a miracle.
Jesus, in his infinite wisdom sent them back to Bethany.
when Lazarus passed, Mary and Martha ran to Jesus and lamented
"had you been here then he would not have died!"
Jesus replied "don't you know he had to die in order for me to perform a miracle? where's the magic in giving life to the living?"
so Jesus went to the tomb where Lazarus lay
and commanded him "Rise up and Walk!"
and he did.
that day, Lazarus became a living testimony that even death can't stop a miracle.

when my father fell sick, I ran to Jesus to tell him the news.
I was expecting a miracle.
Jesus, sent me back to where I'd come from.
when my father died, I ran to Jesus and lamented
"had you been here then he would not have died!"
Jesus replied "don't you know he had to die in order for me to perform a miracle?"
when he came, though, it was not my father he rose from the dead but the part of myself I had buried with him.
I had amputated the parts of myself I thought I could live without reasoning that I could not be whole
and I heard a voice say
"did you not think that I could raise you from the dead?
did you think that just because I waited years to come that I would not make a miracle out of you?
yes, your daddy is dead. but your Father yet lives.
RISE UP AND WALK!

open up your lockjaw mouth and release the winged creatures you have trapped in your chest!
you can still be a poem though he is not here!"
I did not know I could still be a poem when he is not here
I did not know what to be
the Mary and Martha in me did not think I could still be a miracle, but here I stand. The stone rolled away from the tomb.
if you look closely you can still see remnants of bandages on my hands and feet
you can still smell the scent of the grave in my clothes
but know that I am living now.
not even death can stop this miracle.

Ashlee Haze is a poet and spoken word artist from Atlanta by way of Chicago. Earning the nickname "Big 30" because of her consistency in getting a perfect score, she is one of the most accomplished poets in the sport of poetry slam. She has been a part of the Atlanta Poetry circuit for over a decade and has been writing for over 15 years. Ashlee Haze is a 3-time Queen of the South poetry Slam Champion, 2-time Women of the World Poetry Slam Finalist and 2-time National Poetry Slam semi-finalist. She has appeared on NPR's Tiny Desk series alongside Blood Orange. After her poem "For Colored Girls who Don't Need Katy Perry when Missy Elliott is Enough" went viral, Missy Elliott was so moved she showed up at the poet's house. Ashlee is the host of Moderne Philosophy, an educational podcast for creatives.